THE COMMON SENSE CODE GUIDE WITH WISDOM FROM THE AGES

VOLUME I: ILLUMINATION

INSPIRED BY THE ANCESTORS,
WRITTEN BY MALIK EL

Library of Congress Control
Number: 2025907794

ISBN: 979-8-21841611-9

Printed in the United States of America

Dedication

To my ancestors: your strength, wisdom and resilience has shaped my journey and inspired this book. The creation of this book is a tribute to your enduring legacy and the lessons you've passed down through generations. Thank you for lighting the path that I now find myself on.

Table of Contents

Introduction   1

SECTION: 1

           CONSCIOUSNESS RAISING   4

"You Already Have What You Need Inside of You to Succeed"   5

WISDOM FROM THE AGES - I   6

"You Can Be Blind to Reality with Your Eyes Wide Open"   7

WISDOM FROM THE AGES - II   8

"Understanding The Self"   9

WISDOM FROM THE AGES - III   10

"How Your Name Affects You"   11

WISDOM FROM THE AGES - IV   13

"Let Your Intuition Be Your Guide"   14

WISDOM FROM THE AGES - V   16

"Every Day That You Wake Up, You Have Another Chance
and Another Choice – The Two C's"   17

WISDOM FROM THE AGES - VI   18

"Most People Approach Life Based on What Is Offered"   19

WISDOM FROM THE AGES - VII   20

"Don't Unconsciously Throw Your Life Away; It Could Easily
Happen to You, Too"   21

WISDOM FROM THE AGES - VIII   23

"We, The People, Need Some Very Important Questions Answered by
Academia"   24

WISDOM FROM THE AGES - IX   25

"You Were Told to Go Out in The World and Make a Success of Yourself"   26

WISDOM FROM THE AGES - X   28

"What Do I Say to Myself About Myself?"   29

WISDOM FROM THE AGES - XI   31

"Perceived Pressure Can Become a Mental Illness for Some People"   32

WISDOM FROM THE AGES - XII   33

"The Meaning and Purpose of Life"   34

SECTION: 2
      DON'T BE LIKE DUMB DRIVEN CATTLE   35

"Don't be a Follower; Be a Leader"   36

WISDOM FROM THE AGES - XIII   37

"You Have to Take Chances in Life; Otherwise You Won't Get Ahead in Life"   38

WISDOM FROM THE AGES - XIV   39

"There's a Trick to Every Trade"   40

WISDOM FROM THE AGES - XV   42

"Pursue Income Today and Invest Tomorrow"   43

WISDOM FROM THE AGES - XVI   45

"It Could Be So Exciting for You to Make Your Life Story into a Movie Script"   46

WISDOM FROM THE AGES - XVII   47

"You Have to Take Calculated Risks in Life to Make It"   48

WISDOM FROM THE AGES - XVIII   50

"Where There Is a Will, There Is a Way"   51

WISDOM FROM THE AGES - XIX   52

"Nothing Beats a Failure but a Try"   53

SECTION: 3
      THE SECRET CODES   54

"Timing and Rhythm Is The Key to Life"   55

WISDOM FROM THE AGES - XX   57

"Global Warming… or Should It Be Renamed Global Warning?"   58

WISDOM FROM THE AGES - XXI   60

"You Only Have Two Options"   61

WISDOM FROM THE AGES - XXII   62

"The Modern Day Definers of Reality Changed Today's
Marginalized Groups' Historical Perspective of Themselves
from That of Their Ancestor's Perspective and World View"   63

WISDOM FROM THE AGES - XXIII   65

"Acute Ghetto Etiquette"   66

WISDOM FROM THE AGES - XXIV   68

"Don't Just Read a Sign Literally; Read into The Sign to See If
There Is an Underlying Message Behind It"   69

WISDOM FROM THE AGES - XXV   71

"Wake Up! Third-World Countries and Third-World People Never
Existed in Reality"   72

WISDOM FROM THE AGES - XXVI   73

"The Invisible Energy Grid"   74

WISDOM FROM THE AGES - XXVII   75

"What's Happening, Is a Popular Catchphrase and Everyone Wants to
Know What's Happening"   76

SECTION: 4
THE FACULTIES OF YOUR MIND ARE
A TERRIBLE THING TO WASTE

    78

"It's Not About Black Folks Versus White Folks; It's About The Fact
That We, The People, Can't Survive Consuming Alcohol and Illegal Drugs"   79

WISDOM FROM THE AGES - XXVIII   80

"The False Promises Associated with Drinking Alcohol and
Consuming Illegal Drugs"   81

WISDOM FROM THE AGES - XXIX   83

"You Are Essentially Frying Your Brain When You Smoke"   84

SECTION: 5
THE NATURE OF A MAN AND THE NATURE OF A WOMAN 85

"What Are The Consequences for The Average Girl That Allows
Too Many Men to Enter Her Holiest of Holy Places?"   86

WISDOM FROM THE AGES - XXX   87

"The Nature of a Man"   88

WISDOM FROM THE AGES - XXXI   89

"A Man Can't Love a Woman Like a Woman Loves a Man"   90

WISDOM FROM THE AGES - XXXII   92

"A Woman's Greatest Mistake"   93

WISDOM FROM THE AGES - XXXIII   94

"Too Much of a Good Thing Can Be Bad for You"   95

SECTION: 6
YOU ARE IN THE PROBLEM SOLVING BUSINESS
WHETHER YOU KNOW IT OR NOT   96

"It's Better to Be a Problem Solver Than a Problem Maker"   97

WISDOM FROM THE AGES - XXXIV   98

"Avoid The Jealous and Envious People Pretending to Be a
Friend Disease"   99

WISDOM FROM THE AGES - XXXV   100

"Do The Right Thing"   101

WISDOM FROM THE AGES - XXXVI   102

"Warning: Avoid The Confidently Ignorant People Among Us"   103

WISDOM FROM THE AGES - XXXVII   104

"Some People Are Too Damn Lazy to Think for Themselves"   105

WISDOM FROM THE AGES - XXXVIII   106

"You Just Got a Bought-and-Paid-for Lesson in Life"   107

WISDOM FROM THE AGES - XXXIX   109

"The Ultimate Step in Every Decision Making Process"   110

WISDOM FROM THE AGES - XL   111

"You Are The Hero That You Have Been Waiting For"   112

Conclusion   113

About The Author   115

Introduction

The main objective of this book is to have you (the reader) think about common sense in more concise terms and to simultaneously develop a more conscious state of mind. Because many people live and think without using common sense, they simply react to daily situations and may even mimic other people's actions. Although most people are born with the ability to develop common sense, some people do not develop it independently. This book should be used as a guide to begin or continue thinking in more concise common sense terms when it comes to daily living, by applying the knowledge herein. This book is also a survey of common sense terms and phrases, with old adages (wisdom from the ages/old sayings) included to offer examples of common sense thinking and understanding.

The information written herein offers you, the reader, some life lessons and messages within many of the common sense codes and old adages, so take heed of it, if you will.

The topic of common sense is so vast and expansive that we can only approach the subject through particular matters where you would use common sense, along with old adages and their interpretations. With these examples (written in a code form) of common sense applications, the reader may clearly understand the point that is being made in each code.

Here is an example of one of the codes, titled: "Do The Right Thing." It's a popular catchphrase with which most people are familiar. However, most people interpret this phrase to mean different things; ultimately, it's left up to each individual to interpret it for themselves. This particular code, "Do The Right Thing," clearly points out one of the many misconceptions about common sense, just because a phrase is popular doesn't make it a part of a common sense understanding.

The word "common" in the phrase "common sense" refers to the fact that a substantial number of people have the ability to possess common sense. Now, common sense can be thought of as sound judgement in practical matters. Furthermore, common sense is a form of practical decision making, and a common sense understanding offers you the ability to project what the outcome of something may be based on practical matters. Having a common sense understanding can stop people from making irrational mistakes, and it helps them to make sound judgement on what to do and when to do it.

Now, let's again focus on the code titled "Do The Right Thing." Well, this particular phrase (it's a catchy phrase) is not in line with a common sense understanding, because the right thing is subjective. As we may know, doing what is best for a given situation is more conducive to a common sense understanding. Nonetheless, this matter can still be debatable among many people. However, the point has been made here by raising the question in the individual reader's mind about doing the right thing versus doing what is best for a given situation. As we may further understand, common sense dictates that doing what is best for a given situation is more prudent than doing the right thing.

So, this particular code – "Do The Right Thing" – and every code written herein offers the reader an effective action or thought, and every code aligns with a common sense understanding.

Now, at this point, it is worth mentioning the title of this book again, *The Common Sense Code Guide With Wisdom From The Ages Volume - I: Illumination*, because one of the most significant possible benefits of reading this common sense information is that it may lead you to find wisdom by offering you a clear and concise understanding of what common sense really is in particular matters. So, you must know that wisdom is knowledge applied to a particular application of truth. However, you can't find wisdom without first having an understanding of common sense.

Questions may arise about this phrase that is a part of the title, specifically, "With Wisdom From The Ages," this particular phrase refers to the old adages or old common sense sayings that have been shared verbally from generation to generation and have been used to teach common sense within a family unit. Now, this information is in a printed format for you, the reader, to learn, digest, share and study for better comprehension.

This motivational common sense book will raise your awareness about certain concepts considered to be common sense and other concepts that may not be considered common sense..

In essence, this is a book of codes with old adages, and the codes are, by design, written with the intent to work every time each code is employed in a particular manner, if applicable. So, these common sense codes are used as examples to allow for a greater comprehension and a better understanding, and to make sense of many common sense terms, phrases and old adages. This book also challenges the reader to realize what common sense really is, common sense is having a basic knowledge and understanding of the world and moreover sound judgement and practical wisdom. Furthermore, common sense is an individual undertaking and sometimes realizing what common sense is, or is not, in various circumstances can be shocking! So, read on and compare your understanding of common sense to the information written herein.

***

The information written herein is a compilation of individual lessons and messages (common sense codes and old adages) that teaches common sense.

So, when reading this material, it is suggested that you stop after each lesson and message, then digest the information at that point and glean from it for clarity and understanding, then continue reading.

SECTION: 1
CONSCIOUSNESS RAISING

"You Already Have What You Need Inside of You to Succeed"

Are you familiar with the classic story, *The Wizard of Oz*? There are several main characters in the story: Dorothy, the Scarecrow, the Tin Man and the Cowardly Lion. Although there were many other characters in the story, we will focus on the main characters to make the point in this common sense code.

As the classic story unfolds, the main characters assemble to travel down the yellow brick road. Each main character has a goal in mind, which is something that they want and need, and they all think that only the Wonderful Wizard of Oz can provide it. While traveling down the yellow brick road, they encounter obstacles and problems and different situations, as we do in reality. However, when they arrive at their destination (the Land of Oz), they eventually, to their surprise, find out that the Great Wizard of Oz is a fraud. Dorothy, the Scarecrow, the Tin Man and the Cowardly Lion come to the realization that they already have what they need to succeed inside themselves. They just needed to convince themselves of the reality of the matter.

The point of this classic story is that it reminds us that we already have what we need to succeed inside ourselves. It's our individual responsibility and duty to convince ourselves of this reality. If you don't believe that you already have what it takes to succeed, then there is a high probability that no one else will believe it either. When you find yourself in a situation where you don't believe in yourself, then you might as well quit because you can't build if you don't have a foundation to build onto.

So, decide today to convince yourself that you already have what it takes to succeed (this is imperative in order to build the confidence you need to go forth) with whatever goal you choose.

As you think, so shall you be!

WISDOM FROM THE AGES - I

"USING YOUR IMAGINATION
IS A SPIRITUAL SENSATION"

Interpretation: The act or power of forming a mental image of something not present to the senses, or never before wholly perceived in reality, and feeling it come from the power and energy in the universe through you.

"You Can Be Blind to Reality with Your Eyes Wide Open"

We must know that the mind sees through the eyes, and it directs the eyes on what to see. So, seeing reality is not just opening your eyes and looking out – it's more than that. When you look, you must have a focus and an organized plan to decipher the reality of the situation that you are looking at. However, if you have made up your mind that you don't really care to see reality for what it is, then you will, of course, have a different perspective of what reality is or is not.

The typical individual deals with reality by using an efficient and realistic perception. However, some people may try to escape reality; perhaps an unconventional individual may take a different approach – he or she may try to shy away from the challenges that come their way, and maybe reality is too painful for that individual. We must know that there is only one reality and we all experience it from our own extremely different perspectives, although some people may think that they have their own individual reality. However, some people may choose not to deal with reality as it is and this could be for a multitude of reasons. These particular actions can make an individual inefficient when it comes to dealing with reality.

So, here we have a few of the reasons why some people are actually blind to reality with their eyes wide open.

WISDOM FROM THE AGES - II

"SOMETIMES YOU CAN'T SEE THE LESSON IN THINGS UNTIL YOU COME OUT ON THE OTHER SIDE"

Interpretation: If you know every step before it happens, then you could be following someone else's path.

"Understanding The Self"

As soon as you are born into this world, you are given a name, an identity, a religion, a nationality and an economic status, and these become your reality in general terms. You eventually begin to think that that's who you are. At that time, you are unaware that you have choices in the matter of your identity and belief system, and most people continue thinking of themselves in the way handed down to them at birth. Most of us start out by living in rigid situations because of our culture and education, and the opinions, prejudices and biases that are a part of our environment.

We must start thinking outside the box that we live in by reading, traveling and having new experiences. We ultimately need to turn our attention inward to the true self. Eventually, we will need to quiet our mind from all external noise and turn up the volume on our internal guidance system. This will bring us closer to that sense of awareness that we seek and take us beyond our habitual mode of thinking.

Furthermore, you will need to know your true history so that you can make sense of how you got to where you are now, and then, by knowing this information, you will be more informed and can plan your future accordingly.

So, it's imperative that you know who you really are!

WISDOM FROM THE AGES - III

*"KNOWING YOURSELF IS THE
START OF ALL WISDOM"*

Interpretation: It's self explanatory.

"How Your Name Affects You"

The first piece of information that strangers learn about you is a title that was picked for you by your parents, and maybe your parents didn't realize that they were choosing a name for you from a culture other than your own. You must know that what you are called can have a surprising impact on how others see you. A name (you have the right to change your name legally) is used to identify an individual and for all daily communication, and therefore serves as your self concept, especially in relation to other people.

Of course, many things help to influence our personality, but one lasting thing is the name you are called to answer to every day. Your name is a highly personal influence imposed on you from birth, and it usually stays with you throughout life (unless you are conscious enough to change it). It's easy to forget the part that your name plays in this busy, chaotic world. Your name is the most important anchor to your self identity throughout life. At a basic level, your name can reveal details about your culture and other things about your background. Although, whatever your ethnicity may be, and whatever name you may have, if other people can look at you and determine your cultural identity correctly and yet your name does not reflect your true culture, then that makes a statement about you. It could possibly indicate that you may not know your true history and that you may not know that you are dishonoring your own ancestors by being called by a name other than one of your true cultural names.

You may have also noticed that most cultures follow the traditional names of their forefathers and this is one of the ways that they honor their ancestors. They actually honor their ancestors by naming themselves with their own cultural names. Furthermore, some people have been brainwashed into thinking that a name means nothing other than it should be a good Christian name – this type of thinking may not be very advantageous for these particular individuals over a long period of time. However, many cultures around the world look at these people who do not subscribe to their own cultural names and pity them. Because these particular people just don't understand the significance of following in their own traditional cultural names.

Now, do you see how your name can affect you?

Your name can affect you regardless of your income, level of education, creed, gender, etc.

WISDOM FROM THE AGES - IV

"DON'T START SOMETHING THAT YOU
CANNOT END WITH"

Interpretation: Do not initiate or begin anything that you know you cannot handle until its completion – and this refers to relationships with people, places, things and animals.

"Let Your Intuition Be Your Guide"

Most people have the faculty of intuition. However, everyone doesn't have the wherewithal to initiate it and use their intuition to guide them through life's changes and challenges. In everyday life, there is too much confusion, and an overload of information, and far too many decisions that must be made, sometimes within a flash of the moment. This is why we really need to rely on our intuition/internal guidance system and summon it from within for guidance.

To follow your intuition means to follow your internal guidance system – they are the same thing referred to by different names. We can only assume that we all possess some variation of an intuition/internal guidance system, and that it can lead us if we learn to trust it and allow ourselves to follow it.

Here's where we all come to the fork in the road when trying to decide whether to follow our intuition/internal guidance system or some other entity. Some people even refer to their intuition/internal guidance system as their third eye or the God force within. It's all the same power from within you. So, the fork in the road is deciding whether to follow the voice within, your intuition/internal guidance system or a philosophy, a learned belief, another person, or a group of people for guidance. It's a decision that almost everyone must make in life. This is definitely one of the most important decisions a person makes in their lifetime because it can have everlasting effects on your life.

So, another important question is: is it easier to trust yourself with your own guidance, or is it easier to trust some other entity, philosophy or person other than yourself with your guidance?

This fork in the road is a very pivotal point in a person's life. The ancestors taught on this matter, and the information has been passed down from one generation to another. What they taught was for us to always follow our own mind, which means following our own intuition/internal guidance system, regardless of what we have learned to the contrary.

Here's an old saying that relates to this matter that the elders taught: "Let your conscience be your guide." Although it was stated just like that, it meant for you to let your intuition/internal guidance system be your guide.

Definition of intuition: An innate ability to understand something at face value and then let your intuition/internal guidance system guide you without the need for conscious reasoning.

WISDOM FROM THE AGES - V

"AT CERTAIN TIMES YOU HAVE TO STEP
BEYOND THE LIMITATIONS OF YOUR MIND"

Interpretation: Sometimes you may have to go outside of your comfort zone and awareness, and operate on faith and your imagination only.

"Every Day That You Wake Up, You Have Another Chance and Another Choice – The Two C's"

The point being made here is that you have another chance to live again today (that's wonderful!). You also have another choice over what to do with your life today. To reiterate, each and every day that you wake up is the greatest of all gifts, it's another day to live again and the second greatest gift is the gift to choose what you will do today and in the future.

So, be grateful for these wonderful gifts. In contrast, wildlife creatures don't have the great gift of choice; their nature dictates that they operate only from instincts. You must also realize that some people didn't wake up this morning, yet here we are, among the living, and we must know that life is a gift – so rejoice in this day!

Now, the question remains: what will you do with this precious day that is still in your keeping? Well, it comes down to the two C's: another chance and another choice. You should realize that the two C's are a special gift from a higher power than mankind.

You can abuse the gift of the two C's, or you can recognize that you are very fortunate to be alive and should try to add something to society and your community during your time on this planet, because that's what life is about in the grand scheme of things. Is there a rich man or woman on their deathbed who wouldn't trade their fortune today for another opportunity to experience the two C's?

Here we are, enjoying the greatest of all gifts. I can only hope that you realize the value of the immense gift of another chance and another choice, because tomorrow isn't promised to anyone.

WISDOM FROM THE AGES - VI

"THE FUTURE BELONGS TO THOSE
WHO PLAN FOR IT"

Interpretation: It's self explanatory.

"Most People Approach Life Based on What Is Offered"

Yes, most people approach life based on what is offered to them, instead of trying to make life the way they want it to be within their own imagination and willpower. You must realize for yourself that you have the power to choose your own path and the power to change it, too. It seems hard to believe, but that's exactly the fact of the matter. *You have to simply believe in yourself more* (to the maximum in order to get it done)! That's exactly where your power lies; your power is in believing in yourself. You can will what you want into existence when you believe you can.

You don't even need any money to start believing in yourself; money is not your power! Your willpower is your *real* power, and it's generated by how much you believe in yourself and your ability to attain the goals you choose.

So, don't just accept any old thing that is offered to you or that's placed in front of you because you have the power within you to choose, regardless of any perceived lack or limitation. However, this may only happen if you believe you have the power within you to make a change!

WISDOM FROM THE AGES - VII

*"WHEN ONE DOOR CLOSES,
ANOTHER DOOR OPENS"*

Interpretation: When one opportunity ends, another opportunity will present itself.

"Don't Unconsciously Throw Your Life Away; It Could Easily Happen to You, Too"

You may question how anyone could possibly throw their life away. The statement doesn't compute at first, although it makes sense when you comprehend the common sense understanding of it. Basically, "don't unconsciously throw your life away" means that an individual can make a series of bad decisions – one after the other – in a snowball effect. This can be the beginning of the road to hell, due to the accumulation of bad decisions. Thereafter, an individual may find themselves almost totally unable to rebound from the situation caused by the bad choices in their life – perhaps to the point of being incarcerated or something even more detrimental.

For example, a person may start drinking alcohol and/or using illegal drugs for recreational purposes. However, our elders have proven that consuming illegal drugs and alcohol is addictive and that those activities can be a losing game over a really short period of time.

Another losing game is choosing the wrong life partner or mate. They could turn out to be a narcissist and you'll eventually realize that you've made a bad choice of a life partner. As we may know, in the narcissist's mind, it's always about the self.

Another example of how you can unconsciously throw your life away is wholeheartedly believing in things you don't fully understand, such as get rich quick schemes, gambling for a living, religion, etc. These practices can become traps waiting for the unsuspecting naïve person and they are a real equal-opportunity employer for all. Furthermore, the root cause of how many people begin to throw their lives away is by not thinking for themselves as individuals. People tend to follow or mimic what they see other people do. Some people can easily be led into negative situations or circumstances, which is one of the most common ways to throw your life away.

To counter all the negativity you may face in your life, you must be steadfast, focused and goal-oriented. Keep these types of thoughts in the forefront of your mind so that you don't get side-tracked into unconsciously handing your future over to another person, philosophy, entity or religion. So, set goals for yourself and manage yourself until you see your goals manifested. After reaching your goals, set new goals while guiding your life in the direction you want and continue living in that manner. You'll be continuously setting new goals while guiding your life on a path of your choice.

You must realize that your "life is what you make of it" – good or bad, positive or negative.

WISDOM FROM THE AGES - VIII

"IT'S NOT SO MUCH ABOUT WHAT HAPPENS TO YOU IN LIFE, BUT HOW YOU REACT TO IT THAT MATTER'S MOST"

Interpretation: Unexpected situations will occur in your life, however your main focus should be on handling those situations accordingly.

"We, The People, Need Some Very Important Questions Answered by Academia"

It is a fact that colleges and universities charge their students large sums of money for a degree. Well, we, the people, need to know how many degrees of knowledge are involved in receiving a doctorate, a master's degree and a bachelor's degree, etc.?

We must realize that graduates receive a limited degree of knowledge from their academic discipline. However, graduates should be informed about how many degrees of knowledge they are actually receiving from their education. What is the actual degree of knowledge received from each degree? Is it ten degrees, twenty degrees, or three-hundred-and-sixty degrees? Graduates really need and deserve to know what they are paying for, because they assume that they have acquired a high level of knowledge in their particular field of study and may be led to think that they can succeed at the highest levels in their field. This may be the reason why some graduates can't find work in their chosen field of academic discipline – because graduates only have a limited degree of knowledge in a particular field of study, and the university system doesn't inform the student of their limited degree of knowledge until they are closer to employment. The average university's advice after you have already enrolled in a discipline is maybe that you'll need a more advanced education to gain top-level employment in your field.

We, the people, need some very important questions answered by academia.

WISDOM FROM THE AGES - IX

*"IF THE PATH BEFORE YOU IS CLEAR,
THEN YOU'RE PROBABLY ON SOMEONE
ELSE'S PATH"*

Interpretation: If you know every step ahead before it happens, then you could be following someone else's program.

"You Were Told to Go Out in The World and Make a Success of Yourself"

This is the standard experience of most young adults upon graduation from high school or college. Other things may have been suggested, but many older adults tell young adults this same phrase. Furthermore, most commencement speeches reiterate the same message to varying degrees.

Now, even though your parents have been telling you what to do from birth, upon graduation, as a young adult, you are told to go out in the world and make a success of yourself. Your teachers and professors will also share the same message with you, and many older relatives will most likely utter the same phrase as advice.

So, from the beginning, you have been told what to do and when to do it. Then, when you reach young adulthood, they suddenly start saying, "Go out in the world and make a success of yourself." The young person's first thought may be, *How?* This is a very good and timely question, because people have been telling you what to do all of your life up until this point.

You, as the young adult, have got to decide what to do next on your own; you've basically been told it's up to you from here. It's no wonder young people get mixed up and confused after years of being told what to do, then you start hearing "It's up to you from here."

Realistically, most young adults need more time to learn to chart their own direction and set their own goals. A young person in that predicament also needs to learn skills on how to navigate around mean-spirited people and handle the problems that will pop up in their journey. So, it's no wonder that young folks sometimes get off track (from their goals).

The point is that young adults can't help but be confused in this transitional period in their lives. Suddenly, everyone around them is telling them to go out in the world and make a success of themselves. This is especially hard if they've had little to no support from the start – the situation can be totally confusing at that point. Usually, the young person will prefer to think about going out and enjoying themselves.

It appears that when it comes to many young adults' overall transitional period around graduation, it can be a set-up for a false start in their adult lives.

Older adults should stop telling most young adults to go out in the world and make their life a success. Because that type of statement can put too much undue pressure on the young adult. The media (a major influencer) has always portrayed success as fame and fortune, and that message always gets through to the young adult and causes much more confusion. As we all know, it's not very easy to become a success according to the media's definition of success. All of this rhetoric can cause mass confusion for many young adults, who are, at that point in their lives, unsure of themselves, because it's a major transitional period in their life.

WISDOM FROM THE AGES - X

"IF YOU DON'T MAKE TIME TO WORK ON CREATING THE LIFE YOU WANT, YOU'RE GOING TO BE FORCED TO SPEND A LOT OF TIME DEALING WITH A LIFE YOU DON'T WANT"

Interpretation: It's self-explanatory.

"What Do I Say to Myself About Myself?"

Your self-worth is the opinion you have about yourself and the value you place on yourself. It is your answer to the titled question. By answering this question about your self-worth, this will let you know if you think highly of yourself, whether or not you think of yourself as mediocre, or whether you have low self-esteem (if you are honest with your answer, your answer will not be egotistical). The self-worth question is a good test question for your state of mind and it helps with plotting the direction you want your life to go in. Next, ask yourself an additional question: what is the source of your self-worth? Answering this question helps you to check yourself and determine whether or not you have your head in the sky (dreaming) while your feet are on the ground (reality). It's a reality check.

Only you can honestly answer these questions for yourself and doing so may help you to have a deeper understanding of yourself. So, don't try to convince yourself that you are somebody else you may want to be. Who you really are is good enough to succeed at whatever you want to do. If you continue to promote yourself, apply yourself, learn and really work hard at it and practice, you may start to believe that you really can do it and start to excel.

Let's look at Nikola Tesla; he was a great engineer, physicist and inventor, and was truly a self-made man. No one else made him into a great engineer, physicist and inventor; he had to believe that he could achieve these goals. Let's also look at Frank Lloyd Wright Sr., who was a famous architect, designer, writer and educator. He made himself into a very successful businessman with his architectural design philosophy, which promoted buildings that harmonized with their environments and inhabitants. These two great men evidently thought highly of themselves, at least enough to accomplish their goals in life.

The point is that whatever you think your self-worth is, you are good enough to succeed and excel, even though it may sometimes appear that the odds are against you.

Understand this: you are only going to be as great as the thoughts you have about yourself, so it makes sense that you should have a high regard for yourself!

WISDOM FROM THE AGES - XI

"SOMETIMES PEOPLE DON'T WANT TO HEAR
THE TRUTH BECAUSE THEY DON'T WANT
THEIR ILLUSIONS DESTROYED"

Interpretation: It's a human tendency to resist challenging or conflicting information.

"Perceived Pressure Can Become a Mental Illness for Some People"

Perceived pressure can be a strong influence on some people and it can dictate how they operate in everyday life. Perceived pressure can cause an individual's thinking abilities to go haywire or even cause the person to have a mental breakdown from the stress of it all. In some cases, people put unnecessary time constraints (perceived pressure) on themselves to reach their goals or to keep up with the latest fashion, cars, homes, etc.

There are other possible reasons for the perceived pressure that some people experience. Some people think of life as a competition and want to look good at all costs or appear to look smarter than others. Many others think that life is about gaining as many material possessions as humanly possible, even if they don't have the time to enjoy or use all of the things they've accumulated. Furthermore, many others have been trained in schools and universities to follow the path of a so-called career above all else in life, and they make this their top priority.

Now, when people think along these particular trains of thought, they sometimes put unnecessary pressure on themselves to keep up with the pace of whatever it is that they've assigned themselves to. So, they create perceived pressure for themselves by competing – even though other people may not see their perceived pressure. However, certain people definitely experience it, and you can sometimes seemingly notice it by their behavior. In reality, living life is definitely not a competition, although, on the flip side, life is what you make it.

So, the best practice in life is to be cool (don't put unnecessary pressure on yourself) with what you do and do the best you can at all times, if possible. No one can realistically expect you to do anything more than your very best. Maintaining this frame of mind doesn't create any feeling of perceived pressure, but allows you to be much more comfortable with yourself mentally. You'll be practically stress-free in comparison to the perceived pressure that most people assign themselves to unconsciously.

WISDOM FROM THE AGES - XII

"YOUR PERCEIVED PROBLEM MAY NOT BE THE
REAL PROBLEM BUT YOUR REACTION TO THE
SO-CALLED PROBLEM MAY
EVENTUALLY BE THE REAL PROBLEM"

Interpretation: What you think is the problem may not be so, instead, it may be the reaction to the problem that causes the biggest issue.

"The Meaning and Purpose of Life"

Some people think that we, human beings, come from nothing and we will return to nothing when we make our final transition from life. Furthermore, they think it doesn't matter what we do while living this life experience and that there is no right way to live, nor is there a wrong way to live.

On the opposite side of the spectrum, there are the religious philosophies and their doctrines that dictate how man should live. They dictate to their followers and believers about what is supposed to be right and wrong. The doctrines and the canons basically tell them how to conduct themselves on a daily basis, according to their faith and practice.

On the flip side, as an individual with free will and with the natural gift of choice, you can choose to assign your life a meaning and a purpose according to how you see fit.

So, the meaning and purpose of life is for you to assign your life a meaning and a purpose, it's just that simple.

So, when people say or think that life doesn't have a meaning or a purpose, it proves that they haven't done the hard work within to determine it for themselves. It's all within your scope of understanding; it's not in the sky or a philosophy or a religion. You must do the hard work of determining a meaning and a purpose for your life while you still can. However, don't just settle for those mass-produced meanings and purposes in life where one size fits all, because you may regret it when you make your final transition into the afterlife.

SECTION: 2 - DON'T BE LIKE DUMB DRIVEN CATTLE

"Don't be a Follower; Be a Leader"

Many people are in the mindset of waiting for a leader to appear, so that they can be led to the so-called Promised Land. Furthermore, it seems to be a well-established fact worldwide that many more think it's easier to be a follower than it is to be a leader. Those are some of the main reasons why some people make a conscious decision to be followers – they feel more secure being in the background. It appears that the common man and woman may also think that to be a leader, there's much more pressure on the individual. However, it's only perceived pressure and you don't have to allow yourself to feel that pressure. Then, there are others who assume you are required to have a huge ego to be a leader, because you will be placing yourself in the spotlight, but that's not necessarily true.

A true leader should have some sort of vision and be able to create a mission and goals. Leaders should also have the ability to inspire other people to help accomplish the mission and the goals they have set. Furthermore, leaders take charge of situations and circumstances when necessary. These are some standard qualities of a status quo leader.

However, the message here is: "Don't be a follower; be a leader." This means that people should lead themselves individually and make their own decisions based on their own individual guidance, as opposed to following others who may purport to be leaders – because sometimes when people wholly submit to being followers, they may find themselves in precarious circumstances in the process.

So, for your own benefit and security, be your own individual leader.

WISDOM FROM THE AGES - XIII

"BE THE CHANGE YOU WANT TO SEE"

Interpretation: It's self-explanatory.

"You Have to Take Chances in Life; Otherwise You Won't Get Ahead in Life"

If you don't take a chance on yourself, who will? Some people try to live their life by playing it as safe as possible, by working in the same job and for one company until they retire. In the process, they may not realize that there are no big rewards for playing it that safe in life.

Here's a quote from a book written by Iceberg Slim (a Chicago pimp), titled *Pimp: The Story of My Life*: "You have to put some skin in the game, baby, to get something out of it." This means that you must risk something to get something more substantial out of whatever it is you are trying to gain from. That's a simple principle to understand, because you can't get something for nothing. This capitalist society isn't set up that way.

You only get one life, so take a chance on making it a wonderful life for you and your family. Because when you get to the other side of the dirt, you may regret that you were too afraid to try hard enough to make your goals a reality. It's your choice; it's either "the bigger the risk, the bigger the reward" or "no risk, no reward." Ultimately – and as the title states – "you have to take chances in life; otherwise you won't get ahead in life."

WISDOM FROM THE AGES - XIV

"YOU CAN'T WAIT FOR INSPIRATION YOU HAVE TO GO AFTER IT WITH A VENGENCE"

Interpretation: Inspiration for your next big idea may not just pop into your head, you may have to go after it proactively and aggressively, and do the necessary research.

"There's a Trick to Every Trade"

In this code's title, the word "trick" is intended to be used as savvy (know-how). It's not meant to be used as deceitful. So, the interpretation of the title implies that there's a savvy way to do something in every business trade. Loosely stated, the old adage above also refers to clever methods of attracting business or customers.

Also, there are a number of clever or ingenious skills, techniques or methods employed by many people in every industry or profession, as well as businesses in general, to make their work easier and to help them do their jobs more efficiently.

Basically, one main "trick of the trade" that's standard in most businesses is to buy low (wholesale prices) and sell higher (retail prices). This is a general business principle, which is applicable to many businesses, including the real estate industry, retail stores, wholesale markets and derivatives markets (stocks, bonds, indexes, commodities, currencies and interest rates), etc.

Another common "trick of the trade" in every business is centered on expenditures (expenses); the trick is to preserve more of the money that you earn in business versus the expenses. So, the point here is that you should always try to make more money than you pay out. This is the key to every successful business and is called "balancing the books."

Always remember there are exceptions to every rule. For example, the banking business (loans with interest charges) and the service industry sector (businesses that produce services) do not necessarily use the buy-low, sell-high principle. The banking business's "trick of the trade" is to open as many low-interest cash deposit accounts as possible for customers and then loan that same money out to other select customers who want loans (cars, mortgages and personal loans, etc.), with the bank receiving high-interest payments for a profit.

The "trick of the trade" in the service industry sector is to complete work that is useful to their clients, and they don't necessarily rely on the sale of material goods and products to earn a profit. The service industry basically delivers essential services to the public, which are necessary services that many people require.

So, yes, "there is a trick to every trade" and that can be a good thing for most business transactions in general. By employing these processes, they can help you make money and save you money, too. If you really understand these business principles, you could possibly go into business for yourself and use this information to your advantage. You may eventually become a successful entrepreneur!

WISDOM FROM THE AGES - XV

*"YOU MUST KNOW THAT OFTEN THERE IS A
MEETING BEFORE THE MEETING"*

Interpretation: There is often a discussion prior to the actual meeting and it may be without you or without your knowledge. This is how/why the group may be in agreement all of a sudden.

"Pursue Income Today and Invest Tomorrow"

To be successful in today's capitalist society, you'll need a steady income (unless you're already wealthy), and you will need to invest your excess income into building a portfolio of assets that can produce additional income for yourself.

A portfolio of assets is a range of different investments held by an individual – for example, an investment account, precious metals, life insurance policies, land/property, stocks and bonds, and other financial assets. Building a portfolio is relatively easy to start. You are basically just accumulating investment assets that can possibly increase in value. Now, the big idea of building a portfolio is to increase your overall income and net worth. Let's think of your investment portfolio as a pie that's been divided into varying shapes and sizes, each piece representing a different asset that you own. The main focus of building your portfolio is to choose assets that will increase in value in the future.

So, some assets may have a better return on the initial investment than others, and that's okay. You should group your assets into two different types of categories: long-term and short-term. You can expect that the short-term assets are more aggressive (faster growth) compared to the long-term assets. For example: owning an apartment building is more of a long-term investment asset compared to owning shares of stocks. An apartment building or any land that you may own almost always increases in value over a longer period of time. Stocks, bonds, precious metals and derivatives, however, can increase and decrease in a shorter period of time. The point is that you need a variety of different assets that may increase the value of your overall portfolio's performance. Your assets in your portfolio don't have to increase in value at the same rate or time period to make an overall gain in your net worth. Building your portfolio can take place simultaneously, while still employed in a job.

Yes, you could possibly build additional income and wealth, via the accumulation of assets in your portfolio. However, you will need to increase your income above and beyond your living expenses to have the available money to invest. Another option could be to reduce your living standard and cut back on your living expenses so that you have the money available to invest in assets and build a portfolio, and thereby attaining a secure future for you and your family. So, "pursue income today and invest tomorrow."

WISDOM FROM THE AGES - XVI

*"A BIRD IN THE HAND IS WORTH MORE THAN
TWO IN THE BUSH"*

Interpretation: When you have something of value in your possession now, it's far better and more valuable to you than the promise of twice as much in the future.

"It Could Be So Exciting for You to Make Your Life Story into a Movie Script"

You could possibly entertain yourself by creating a movie script or television script based on your life story and many of the exciting things that you've done in your life. Furthermore, you could also begin to write about what fascinates you most in life and document it as a part of your production. So, whenever you feel as though something is driving you to move – a feeling that's motivating you to act – act on it and document it because it can be a part of your movie script or television script. At times like this, you must enter the theatre of your mind, as your script is already being unfolded and developed from within your imagination, motivated by thoughts and feelings that drive you to act. You just have to remember to write it down and accumulate notes for your script. All you have to do is get your mind and motivation together simultaneously to create the script you want to see in your production.

This type of production may be way more exciting and rewarding compared to just sitting there watching the same old type of movies or television shows all the time. You will be living life to the fullest by being action-oriented and writing your own script for your production, especially if you become lucky enough to produce and direct it yourself.

Most of those Hollywood movies and television shows have a few basic premises, such as boy-meets-girl with a lot of sexual innuendos. There are a lot of movies and television shows with senseless killings and they will throw in a high-speed chase, too, for a change of pace. There may be a Cinderella-type story, too, as well as comedy and adventure movies, etc. However, the point is that we have seen these types of shows over and over again, but no one has seen a movie based on *your* life story.

The message is clear: you should start to write your own movie script or television script and see where it takes you! This could be a game-changing idea, and it's really a fantastic idea compared to you just sitting there and continuing to watch the same old stereotypical movies and television shows.

WISDOM FROM THE AGES - XVII

*"WHAT YOU ARE LOOKING FOR MAY BE RIGHT
IN FRONT OF YOUR FACE"*

Interpretation: What you seek may be in plain sight.

"You Have to Take Calculated Risks in Life to Make It"

If you just go along with the program that's placed in front of you daily, then you will work for the rest of your life just to make a living. The status quo states that you should go to college and get a so-called good education so that you can get a good job. Under that program, you then wind up with a heavy student loan debt to strap you down. By the time you graduate and get a so-called good job, you may have started a family and need a house. That's where the mortgage notes come into play and strap you back down again or, worse, you may continue to rent an apartment (a zero-sum game). So, you may find yourself in a bind if you go about your life following the status quo program. Don't forget about the car payments and car insurance premiums due, and the late charges, etc.

There is a way out of this standard predicament: "You have to take calculated risks in life to make it." You should adopt the mindset of making your money work for you instead of always working for your money. You must change your thinking about how you gain income. There is no law that says you have to always work for your money, when you should be able to see clearly that it's time to make your money work for you. It is essential that you invest your money, perhaps into a particular type of business or businesses that will generate a continuous profit for you in the future.

What's hot now to invest in – the stock market, the commodities market, the real estate market, tax liens, precious metals, etc.? Even if you just start buying and selling on the internet, it's a start. It's all a risk, but you have to calculate how much of a risk you can handle. Now more than ever, "you have to take calculated risks in life to make it."

You can clearly see that a job isn't going to make your dreams come true and it's not designed for that anyway. All employers do is pay you enough to keep you coming back and forth every day and every week. "You have to take calculated risks in life to make it."

You have to find a way to invest in the economy that you already work for, or you will be working for it for the rest of your life. The answer is clear: "You have to take calculated risks in life to make it."

WISDOM FROM THE AGES - XVIII

"YOU'VE GOT TO MAKE A WAY
OUT OF NO WAY"

Interpretation: You have to find a way to succeed at whatever it is that you are trying to do and it may have to be done against all odds.

"Where There Is a Will, There Is a Way"

Your willpower is a major mental faculty that's available to you to employ at any time. It's imperative that you use it for your benefit. You have an unlimited amount of willpower within, so if you have a goal set in your mind, you should reach for it and say to yourself "this will be mine." Then, prove it to yourself by manifesting those things through your will. In real terms, your determination is actually your *will* to do something, and it is better to develop your *will* than to increase your intellect (this is what you should be working on – changing your thinking, for better results).

Tell yourself every day: "Through my willpower, I will do what I want so that I can get what I want."

Willpower is also the mental energy that you develop by using it, so get busy! Always remember: "Where there is a will, there is a way." In essence, anything is possible if you have the determination.

WISDOM FROM THE AGES - XIX

"NO DOESN'T ALWAYS MEAN NO"

Interpretation: Just because one or two or three people (or more) told you no, it doesn't mean that you should let that be the final answer on the matter, if it's important enough to you.

"Nothing Beats a Failure but a Try"

You are definitely going to fail at something – and you may fail a million times or more. Failure is inevitable, but don't give up. The key is to keep trying because you don't really fail until you quit.

Don't wallow in your misery and don't take the time to feel sorry for yourself. If you fall in life, get back up, brush yourself off and continue on your journey, because "nothing beats a failure, but a try."

SECTION: 3 - THE SECRET CODES

"Timing and Rhythm Is The Key to Life"

Have you ever seen a Double Dutch jump rope routine? It is based on timing and rhythm, just like a woman's menstrual cycle is based on the timing and the rhythm within her body. Another example is the planets in this galaxy (solar system). Now, the Earth spins on its axis while continuing to orbit around the sun. Meanwhile, the Earth will tilt at a particular time, causing it to be a little closer to the sun, which is called summertime. Then, at another point in time, the Earth will tilt in the opposite direction away from the sun while still slowly rotating on its axis, and this is referred to as wintertime. Of course, there's also the spring equinox and the fall equinox, which are all based on timing and rhythm. The entire universe's functions are based on timing and rhythm.

We must understand that metaphysics indicates that what is above is also below, which means that timing and rhythm is in space as well as on the Earth. So, timing and rhythm cycles are a part of our daily lives, whether we know it or not. For example, some people will call being at the right place at the right time a stroke of luck, but that is not luck. Even when it comes to decision-making, timing and rhythm come into play.

Sometimes, you are able to feel the timing of things by the rhythm you may feel in everything that you do. Your body may not verbalize the actual words, but it will give you a mental indication that you should pay attention to certain things and interpret it for yourself, in terms of realizing it is time for a particular thing or action. If you experience this, you may have the ability to know if your timing and rhythm are right. Although it takes time to develop this ability, and everyone may not be able to recognize this gift, you should continue to try to acquire this ability.

It is imperative to feel the timing and rhythm of things to come. There may have been times when you felt that something happened too soon – timing-wise and rhythm-wise, it felt slightly off.

The point is that everything in life works on timing and rhythm and we need to keep this in the forefront of our minds when we're analyzing our thoughts and decisions. Therefore, you should always look at life through the lenses of timing and rhythm, because you may see patterns in life's occurrences and situations that you can take advantage of by feeling the timing and the rhythm.

WISDOM FROM THE AGES - XX

*"SOMETIMES, YOU MAY TRY TO MOVE FASTER
THAN YOUR SHADOW. HOWEVER, THINK
FIRST, BECAUSE, AT CERTAIN TIMES, YOU MAY
NEED TO LET THE RIVER
DEVELOP IT'S NATURAL COURSE"*

Interpretation: At certain times in your life, you may have moved too fast for your own good, when perhaps you should have let certain developments take their natural course.

"Global Warming… or Should It Be Renamed Global Warning?"

The phrase "global warming" refers to the temperatures increasing on planet Earth, but to what extent are the temperatures rising? Answer: The Earth's climate will eventually be far too hot for people to exist on this planet.

According to the ancient ancestors who created the "zodiacus" – A.K.A. the zodiac and more widely recognized today as astrology. It is written in the ancient zodiacus (zodiac) that the Earth's temperatures will continue to rise as this planet creeps closer and closer to the sun in its orbit. All other planets in this solar system will also continually orbit the sun while incrementally moving closer and closer to the sun, while the high temperatures continue to increase. The science of the zodiacus states that all of the planets in this solar system are like magnets being drawn closer and closer by the magnetic pull of the sun and all of the planets will eventually be absorbed into the sun (that's how powerful the sun is). This is why planet Earth is experiencing extreme temperatures and abnormal weather patterns more frequently. Over a period of time, this planet will be uninhabitable because of its close proximity to the sun and the earth will face its inevitable absorption into the sun.

So, it's not as simple as just a little global warming (greenhouse emissions); in fact, it will eventually result in the total destruction of the planet Earth!

Lately, we're hearing more information about increasing space travel and we can see the evidence in the media. People are starting to realize that the inevitable annihilation of this planet is going to take place. There is an international scramble in space to find a planet that can support human life; it will most likely be the moon (because of its proximity to the Earth), or possibly Mars because both planets have a possible water source.

The people who are in charge of worldly affairs do not have the scientific knowledge available nor do they have the capability to change the trajectory of this planet – or any other planet – from the eventual destruction that's going to take place in the solar system.

No worries, though, the total destruction of this planet won't happen in the lifetime of the baby boomers. However, it will eventually be too hot to live on this planet and the future doesn't look bright for our posterity existing on Earth indefinitely.

So, global warming is the beginning of the end of life as we know it on this planet – that's how serious this matter is. "Global warming… or should it be renamed global warning?"

WISDOM FROM THE AGES - XXI

"YOU DON'T MISS YOUR WATER UNTIL YOUR
WELL RUNS DRY"

Interpretation: You don't miss something until you no longer have it available.

"You Only Have Two Options"

Has anyone ever told you that "you only have two options?" If so, then whoever told you that may have been attempting to limit your thinking by trying to limit your options. In reality, you have an unlimited number of options to choose from, although, realistically, you have as many options as you can possibly think of in a given period of time.

So, when someone tells you, "You only have two options, it's a sign for you to start thinking of all the possible options that are available to you for that particular matter.

Don't allow anyone to limit your thinking by attempting to limit your options.

WISDOM FROM THE AGES - XXII

"NEVER INTERRUPT YOUR ENEMY WHEN HE IS MAKING A MISTAKE"

Interpretation: It's self explanatory.

"The Modern Day Definers of Reality Changed Today's Marginalized Groups' Historical Perspective of Themselves from That of Their Ancestor's Perspective and World View"

Some of the most well recognized indigenous ancient ancestors were known in history as the Moors, the Nubians, the Carthaginians, the Zulu, etc. (original names of indigenous people prior to the fifteenth century). Today, the descendants of these ancient ancestors are labeled as Black, Negro, Colored, African, African American, etc. However, the modern-day definers of reality have the marginalized groups of today identifying with these labels because they have been blinded to the reality of their situation. Can you see how they have changed the perspective of today's marginalized groups? The marginalized groups are also losing more of their native languages, which are being replaced with English, French and Spanish.

Furthermore, today's marginalized groups unconsciously name their children with names from other cultures (to their own detriment), as they were taught by religious missionaries that these were good Christian names to have.

What about the world view of today's marginalized groups? Has it been changed from that of their ancient ancestors' worldview? Well, according to the modern-day definers of reality, the new year begins on January 1st. every year. However, the indigenous ancient ancestors looked at nature and determined that the new year begins during the spring equinox (nature begins a renewed life cycle on approximately March 21st), so there we have a paradox.

Some people may think this information doesn't make a difference in their lives, and that it's useless to even mention it. This may be so to the modern-day definers of reality or even an unconscious mind, but everyone needs to know the truth. They may ask, "What's the point of all of this information?" The answer is: "Can you see how they've changed the perspective and worldview of the marginalized groups of today?"

It's no surprise that these marginalized groups of today are victimized regularly; every other culture can clearly see they're easy targets for abuse. They haven't been allowed to freely maintain any significant form of leadership, power or cohesion as a culture since the ancient Punic Wars. It's also due to the all-out war (labeled the transatlantic slave trade) or wars waged against them during the late fifteenth century, which is still silently and subtly continuing today and is now called, "The System of White Supremacy."

Today's marginalized groups have been totally mortified, confused and misled by the modern-day definers of reality. They are in a very peculiar predicament in the world today. However, they should not be dismayed nor should they be confused. They should just follow the logic that came into existence with the universe, in all circumstances.

WISDOM FROM THE AGES - XXIII

"THE BEST FORM OF DEFENSE IS A GOOD OFFENSE"

Interpretation: When you are on the attack, it is actually offense and defense at the same time.

"Acute Ghetto Etiquette"

It may be that you don't know where you are or who you really are, and you don't have a clue about any goals or dreams for yourself. You might be living day by day by the grace of the Lord. All that you think you know is that "this ghetto ain't no slum" (there is a distinction between a "ghetto" and a "slum"). You may be living on Section 8 housing assistance and food stamps or The Electronic Benefits Transfer (E.B.T.). You may even have yourself enrolled in The Women, Infants & Children program (W.I.C.) to help support your little babies with their milk and baby formula.

You are unconscious of the fact that every able body should be capable of supporting itself. So, you've turned a blind eye to your living conditions, with roaches in the front room, rats in the back and gangsters in the alleyway with baseball bats. Your entertainment is having several baby daddies coming and going at the same time and you think it's fun. Your general attitude is "I don't care what anyone else thinks about me, because they don't make my toilet flush." You justify your situation by telling yourself it could be worse.

When you think in a "ghetto fabulous" manner, you get more of the same conditions; you bring these circumstances on yourself with your thoughts! The explanation of "acute ghetto etiquette" is proof that it's all in your thinking, positive or negative, although you have a choice in the matter, and it always begins with your thoughts.

However, to be successful, you must see yourself reaching the goals and dreams that you have set for yourself and believe you can achieve them. Then, immediately, your mind will start to wonder, "How in the world am I going to make all this happen?"

Well, first of all, you must believe that you can make your goals and dreams come true. If you can't convince yourself that you will reach your goals and dreams, it's most likely not going to happen for you, because no one is going to do it for you. Otherwise, without positive thoughts and positive goals, and belief that you will achieve, you'll be back to settling for what some people think is the easy life – "acute ghetto etiquette" or some variation of it.

WISDOM FROM THE AGES - XXIV

"WHEN YOUR BED GETS HARD IN ONE SPOT,
THEN YOU SHOULD PICK UP YOUR BAGS
AND WALK"

Interpretation: If you are experiencing constant problems in the area you live, and getting answers that don't make any sense, and every answer you get is wrong for your situation, you should move away from there.

"Don't Just Read a Sign Literally; Read into The Sign to See If There Is an Underlying Message Behind It"

There is an old adage that states, "A picture is worth a thousand words." This can sometimes apply when reading signs in public view. If you pay close attention to certain signs, billboards, news headlines, certain advertising on the internet and church marquee signs and directories outside on the lawn etc., there may be another message implied within the same sign! It's evident that there is a system being used to get messages out to those people in the "in-crowd," because how would people in the "in-crowd" know to think along the same lines without having any meetings?

It is an established fact that everyone won't pay attention to the underlying messages on display right in front of them. So, the people that send the messages don't have to concern themselves with whether everyone realizes what is taking place with this form of communicating messages. This is not a conspiracy theory; it's a part of reality. Please pay closer attention in the future to the many different billboards – for example, one billboard may state a part of a message, then – when you drive down the road a little further – a second billboard completes the sentence (for those aware of this form of communicating messages).

There are other methods used, such as when news articles have a headline that states one thing clearly, then the article itself discusses something totally different (there may be a message in the confusion). The average person may not think anything of it if they're not familiar with this form of communicating messages in public view. Always remember: "There may be more to it than meets the eye."

These are some of the subtle ways that messages are sent in plain sight for people to read and receive without everyone realizing what's actually taking place. However, there are many other methods of getting messages to people in plain sight, and those messages may go unnoticed by people who are not familiar with this particular form of communicating messages.

So, don't just read a sign verbatim; think about what other implications a sign may convey by reading more deeply into it, especially peculiar signs that may seemingly have an underlying message.

WISDOM FROM THE AGES - XXV

*"WHAT'S DONE IN THE DARK WILL
EVENTUALLY COME INTO THE LIGHT"*

Interpretation: The things that people do in secret will eventually be
revealed.

"Wake Up! Third-World Countries and Third-World People Never Existed in Reality"

Past global politicians created the phrase, "Third World." This phrase may have been used as a code word to classify certain groups of people that the global politicians wanted to remain in a permanent underclass group. It seems to emphasize the message that the members of the North Atlantic Treaty Organization (NATO) would remain in a dominant position to exploit the so-called Third-World people. In reality, there is no such thing as a Third World or a Third-World people, because there is only one world that exists in our known reality and it is within this third dimension that we live. However, certain people with an extremely conservative mindset may lay claim to being superior to all other people on this planet. Therefore, in their philosophy of mind, they come first before all other people, particularly the indigenous people of the planet.

The phrase "Third World" seems to imply that there must also be a "First World" and a "Second World," too. Of course, according to the extreme conservative mindset, we must assume that the First World would, in general, be considered the whole of Europe, North America and parts of Australia. The Second World, we must assume, would most likely include all of the communist countries, and the Third World could possibly consist of all other people on this planet classified as non-white or people with color in their skin.

However, progressive people should not think in terms of Third-World classifications or Third-World countries, because that phrase is a global political fabrication and is used to relegate particular people to a permanent underclass. So, the latest global political phrase being used today – in an attempt to circumvent the phrase, the "Third-World countries" and the "Third-World people" – is now stated as the "Developing Countries of the World."

So: "Wake up! Third-world countries and third-world people never existed in reality."

WISDOM FROM THE AGES - XXVI

*"ALWAYS REMEMBER, WHERE THERE IS A
KNOCK, THERE IS A BOOST"*

Interpretation: This statement is used to inspire people when they are faced with adversity. It's also a reminder that something positive can happen after the fact of the matter.

"The Invisible Energy Grid"

Information about the constant invisible energy grid here on Earth is not widely known to the general public. This energy grid flows, crosses and intersects with other energy grid lines in certain locations on the Earth's surface where major cities and smaller cities are located. This is why these cities around the world are located where they are located – it's not by chance; it's because of the intersecting energy grid system. People are drawn in mass to the energy centers that we call "major cities" because they receive energy from the Earth's surface in these locations. This constant energy creates more human activity in these cities worldwide compared to many other locations outside the intersecting energy grid system. The locations of all the major cities in the world are where the major intersecting points on the energy grid system are located.

So, should you move to one of these intersecting points where there is a higher energy frequency to receive more energy and to be more productive? Is there proof of more human activity in these high-energy intersecting centers? The proof is that there is more productivity in these major energy centers, more building construction and more development in general. Also, there is much more socialization in these energy centers and plenty more commercial activity in comparison to areas where the energy grids do not intersect.

Most people do not realize that there is an energy grid system on the planet from which they can benefit. So, people not only receive energy from the sun's rays, but they also receive energy from the Earth's surface (the energy grid) in particular locations on the planet.

This information is not to be confused with the Earth's magnetic field.

WISDOM FROM THE AGES - XXVII

"ACTION SPEAKS LOUDER THAN WORDS"

Interpretation: Physical actions are more concrete than mere conversation about what's going to be done.

"What's Happening, Is a Popular Catchphrase and Everyone Wants to Know What's Happening"

This code will attempt to explain a conversational exercise about "what's happening?" and what should be most important to a young adult — and, yes, it's part of a common sense understanding to want to know what's happening. Ask any young adult in today's American culture, "What's happening?" and they will probably answer, "Nothing much" or "Nothing has been going on lately." Furthermore, many young adults may respond by mentioning events that professional sports teams are having and events in the entertainment industry, or maybe current political events. Some young adults may respond to the statement as a question or as a greeting of sorts: "What's happening?" They may repeat the same statement back to you in response.

To a certain degree, most people think of this catchphrase as a greeting of sorts. However, the distinction that is being made here is to point out what's really happening. So, let's say you ask a young adult if they know what's happening. When you ask that question or make that statement, the average young adult will answer in the affirmative by saying, "Yes, I know what's happening." Younger adults don't want to admit that they don't know what's happening. Then press the issue a little further by asking, "Do you really know what's happening?" Ask that young adult to tell you exactly what they think is happening. The average young adult may start to name all sorts of events and people, places and things that are going on outside of themselves. However, for clarity and to drive the point home, press even further and say to the young person that's not what's happening. Then continue to press the issue again and again about what's happening to the point of annoyance. The individual may stifle their self at this point in the conversation and then may ask you to tell them what you think is happening. Now you have their full attention and they're most likely in a serious mood. Then, you drop a bomb on them by telling them what's really happening. You should answer, "What's happening is what you, the individual, makes happen in your life for yourself." Tell them it's not the things going on outside of themselves (which they named when you initially asked them this question). You tell

76

the young adult that that's what's happening for those particular people involved in those events or activities.

At this point, you may have the individual thinking very seriously and questioning their own intelligence on the matter of what's happening and that's good – to the point that they may rethink what's really happening with them as an individual (this is the result you want). They may also rethink their priorities. This type of scenario can sometimes cause a person to reevaluate their thinking process and also get that individual to realize what's really happening and what's most important to them at the same time. So, the answer to the question "What's happening?" is what you make happen for yourself, rather than what's happening outside of yourself.

This exercise will help a young adult determine whether or not they are focused on their self, as opposed to focusing on things outside of their self.

SECTION: 4 - THE FACULTIES OF YOUR MIND ARE A TERRIBLE THING TO WASTE

"It's Not About Black Folks Versus White Folks; It's About The Fact That We, The People, Can't Survive Consuming Alcohol and Illegal Drugs"

Illegal drug use and alcohol consumption take away from your life and good health. These substances do not add anything to the quality of your life over a long period of time, although those substances can be a temporary escape from your problems, only temporary.

How many people have to make their final transition into the afterlife due to the consumption of these substances before the rest of us get the message? This is how it's set up; it's almost always readily available for you at prices almost anyone can afford, in good times and in bad times, too. Illegal drugs and alcohol are there for you to add to your own demise.

You have to be very foolish to consume illegal street drugs and alcohol and pay for it, knowing it will eventually add to your demise. This particular situation has been proven time and time again.

It doesn't matter to the person selling you the illegal drugs and alcohol. It doesn't matter whether you're black or white, you'll still get the same results – sickness and eventually death. However, it should matter to you.

WISDOM FROM THE AGES - XXVIII

"IT'S BLACK AND WHITE; WE, THE PEOPLE,
CAN'T SURVIVE DRINKING ALCOHOL AND
USING ILLEGAL DRUGS"

Interpretation: It's a proven fact, you/we won't live a long, healthy life using illegal street drugs and alcohol.

"The False Promises Associated with Drinking Alcohol and Consuming Illegal Drugs"

We should all attempt to expose the general public to the lies associated with drinking alcohol and using illegal drugs. The movies, television shows and the media show scenes of people using illegal drugs and drinking alcohol and make it appear enjoyable, pleasurable and cool. Illegal drugs and the drinking of alcohol are always associated with partying, fun and excitement (false promises) in the media and Hollywood. They even portray alcohol consumption as a way to relax and treat ourselves to the good life (false promises).

In most cultures around the world, it's traditional to celebrate with the drinking of alcohol (there is no nutritional value in the consumption of alcohol). However, in reality, we know that illegal drugs and alcohol are killing people at an alarming rate! We see a totally different picture in the reality of drinking alcohol and illegal drug use compared to what the media and Hollywood portrays. The regular consumption of illegal drugs and alcohol deteriorates the consumer's quality of life, as well as that of many people around them.

We have a responsibility to our posterity to ensure that serious warnings are in place about the real dangers of alcohol and illegal drugs. We must try to make sure that everyone – both now and in the future – is aware of the detrimental facts of using illegal drugs and alcohol. It can be a bought-and-paid-for lesson in life, which will reveal itself in the future. Life doesn't have to be lived this way if we warn people that alcohol and drugs can cause major health issues over the long term and can lead to premature death.

More people are waking up to reality and realizing that your state of happiness is in your own mind. Furthermore, happiness is under each individual person's control and without the use of alcohol and illegal drugs. All that is required of you is a shift in how you see yourself being happy. It's either that you see yourself drinking and using drugs to be happy, or you see yourself with your mind clear and on the natural high that life provides when you are thinking correctly!

So, should you drink alcohol and consume illegal drugs, or not drink alcohol and not consume illegal drugs? This is a very serious question that you need to answer for yourself.

WISDOM FROM THE AGES - XXIX

*"EVEN ALCOHOLICS AND DRUG ADDICTS CAN
TEACH YOU SOMETHING"*

Interpretation: When you pay attention to an alcoholic or drug addict, you may learn something, even if it's what not to do with your life.

"You Are Essentially Frying Your Brain When You Smoke"

It's a health hazard when you smoke anything – cigarettes, drugs, etc. Everyone has a pineal gland located near the center of their brain. It is written that the pineal gland activates when the sun's rays enter through the retina in your eyes. The Sun's rays actually travel forward from your retina to your pineal gland and causes a secretion (melatonin) to form around your pineal gland, thus activating enlightenment in your mind. It is worth mentioning that this is a reason not to wear sunglasses, as they block the sun's rays from entering your retina and may cause the pineal gland not to activate properly by blocking the sun's rays (which would naturally cause your pineal gland to activate).

However, when you smoke any substance, the hot smoke not only fills your lungs, but it also fills your brain. In essence, the hot smoke raises the temperature of your brain area. The hot smoke that enters your brain will eventually cause the secretion that usually forms around your pineal gland to stop forming, and on a continuing basis this action begins to dampen your enlightenment process.

The brain was not meant for hot smoke to enter it. The hot smoke that does enter the brain can eventually stop the brain from functioning normally. The hot smoke can calcify the pineal gland over time, therefore limiting your enlightenment and, in essence, frying your pineal gland every time you smoke.

SECTION: 5 - THE NATURE OF A MAN AND THE NATURE OF A WOMAN

"What Are The Consequences for The Average Girl That Allows Too Many Men to Enter Her Holiest of Holy Places?"

The first man that the average girl loves is her father. A little girl will try to please her father by bringing him his favorite newspaper or magazine or his house shoes, so that he will be more comfortable. Thereafter, the average girl gets a little boyfriend in grade school and she thinks she's in love (no physical relations). Although she's heartbroken because the grade school relationship doesn't last, the average girl gets another boyfriend at, perhaps, middle school age. She gets her first kiss and thinks she's in love again for sure, but it's over before she knows it.

By the time the average girl is in high school, she may have experienced a physical relationship. Now, she definitely feels she's in love, however again it doesn't last. The average girl is heartbroken once again. Thereafter, the average girl is in her early twenties and falls in love with someone she thinks is a mature man. She gets her heart broken again! Maybe when the average girl gets closer to the age of thirty, she gets married, only to get her heart broken one more time. The average girl moves on to other relationships and, again, heartbreak.

At a certain point, so many men have entered into her holiest of holy places, with each man spraying his sperm and chromosomes into her, which she absorbs into her bloodstream. She adapts and clings to each man until the point of final heartbreak. Thereafter, the average girl can't adapt any longer or cling to any one man again after all the heartbreak and disappointment and semen. From that point on, her attitude may be that a man will never break her heart again. So, she will go on to other relationships, but her heart and emotions are no longer deeply involved in the relationships.

The message here is that when the average girl allows too many men to enter into her holiest of holy places and she gets her heart broken repeatedly, she can't seem to adapt or attach herself to any one man again. This can be the consequences of the average girl's actions.

WISDOM FROM THE AGES - XXX

*"WHY DO YOU GET THE SAME LESSON OVER
AND OVER AGAIN? IT'S BECAUSE YOU
HAVEN'T LEARNED THAT LESSON YET"*

Interpretation: You may get the same lesson or lessons again and again
until you learn what it is that you need to know.

"The Nature of a Man"

A man's physical body produces about six gallons of semen over his lifespan. Now, semen aids in the creation of life, so it is priceless in terms of value in life. Furthermore, the more semen that a man reserves, the more energy he can generate throughout his lifetime. A man's penis is the representative symbol for sperm, and the ankh uses the penis as part of its symbolism and depiction. The ankh itself represents the eternal symbol of life. The top section of the ankh has an oval shape – the oval shape is a representation of a woman's womb – and the two sidebars that extend out from the center of the ankh represent the woman's fallopian tubes. The long shaft that extends downwards from the center of the ankh represents a man's phallus (penis). This is why the symbolic meaning of the ankh is the eternal symbol of life. The ankh depicts the physical creation of life.

We must surmise that the ankh was created as a symbol to show that a man's phallus and in sequence with a woman's womb and fallopian tubes can create life.

So, should today's man indiscriminately waste this precious life force on mere entertainment (casual sex)? Instead, man should use his sperm for its intended purpose, which is to aid in the creation of life and to give him more energy over his lifespan, so that he may add value to life.

WISDOM FROM THE AGES - XXXI

"A MAN'S GLORY IS HIS WOMAN/WIFE"

Interpretation: A man takes great pride and pleasure in his woman/wife when he is really in love with her.

"A Man Can't Love a Woman Like a Woman Loves a Man"

The above statement is correct, because a man can't physically feel what a woman feels inside her body. A man's physical body is biologically different compared to that of a woman's physical body. For example, when a man and a woman copulate, the man enters the woman's body with his phallus and sprays semen into her vagina. The woman usually absorbs the semen from the man with his chromosomes attached, and the semen and chromosomes travel throughout her physical body via the bloodstream. This is part of how the woman physically feels the man that enters her body. The man's semen travels through the woman's bloodstream and attaches inside the woman's brain and many other body parts, so the woman is able to actually feel that attachment in her physical body.

We should also consider the emotional attachment that a woman feels along with the sexual experience. Then compare that to how a woman may feel about a man without ever having had any sexual experience with him. These are two totally different feelings and the woman is able to physically recognize this difference.

On the other side of the situation, the man, after having a sexual experience with the woman, sometimes develops an emotional attachment to the woman. However, he does not have a physical attachment to the woman, because the bodily fluids that the woman generates do not enter the man's body. The man just showers off all of the woman's bodily fluids. Therefore, the man does not feel the woman inside his body in the same way that the woman physically feels the man. He cannot – it's physically impossible. The man develops more of an emotional attachment to the woman because he sees the woman as trying to please him and give him pleasure at the same time, and the man gets emotionally attached to the pleasing and pleasurable experiences and starts to feel that he wants more of this from the woman.

So, no, a man cannot love a woman like a woman loves a man, because they are biologically different.

WISDOM FROM THE AGES - XXXII

"A WOMAN'S HAIR IS HER GLORY"

Interpretation: A woman's hair is part of her magnificence and her great beauty that she sees.

"A Woman's Greatest Mistake"

A woman's greatest mistake is thinking and feeling that she can change a man with enough love; no woman possesses that kind of power on this planet. Although some women still want to believe they can change a man because of the fantasies or images in their mind, the man has to want to make that change himself or it will not happen. There are no ifs, ands or buts about it.

If you want true love, then both partners should try to communicate openly and truthfully, and be honest about what each partner wants and expects. Communicating with one another will help the relationship to last for the long term and you may have a real possibility of a potential true love.

Another possible way a woman can affect real positive change in a man is to try to grow into love at the same pace as him. With this kind of arrangement, there is a balance between the two individuals. However, do not make a woman's greatest mistake of believing that, with enough love, a woman can change a man, because there's not that much love in this world.

WISDOM FROM THE AGES - XXXIII

"A WOMAN WHO GIVES BIRTH TO A CHILD HAS DELIVERED HER PART IN LIFE'S PLAN"

Interpretation: When a woman gives birth to a baby, she contributes to humanity.

"Too Much of a Good Thing Can Be Bad for You"

Some people act as though they can't get enough of a good thing called love. They watch the television shows about love; they go to the movie theatres to see love stories. They may even listen to love songs on the radio regularly. They are most likely seeking this type of romantic fantasy in their own relationship, hoping to find the perfect love they've seen on the screen. Some people really believe that they will find this perfect love and it will automatically transport them into a blissful wonderland.

However, too many people take this romantic fantasy too far, by seemingly making themselves look foolish to the point that they lose their identity in their love relationship. Romantic love stories can be harmful to many romantics at heart, because they really want the fairytale to come true and it never does.

For many of the so-called glamorous romantic love relationships that many people seek, it can become a nightmare when the fantasy does not match the reality. Is this how life is supposed to work or should we keep our composure and balance in everything that we do in life?

SECTION: 6 - YOU ARE IN THE PROBLEM SOLVING BUSINESS WHETHER YOU KNOW IT OR NOT

"It's Better to Be a Problem Solver Than a Problem Maker"

Some people constantly talk about the problems in their lives and continue to talk about the problems in the world today. This is because they sometimes don't know what else to talk about and their constant negative conversations bring more problems their way. They can't seem to understand that they are creating more problems by constantly talking about the problems.

Life gives each and every one of us an ample amount of problems on a daily basis. This seems to be a part of life that we all must deal with. So, understand the point that is being made here; if you just begin to focus on learning how to solve problems, you may not create new problems. You'll have more important things on your mind, like problem solving. So, instead of unconsciously talking about the problems and bringing more problems your way, change your conversation to problem solving.

Here's a formula that may help to solve some of your problems: The process of "What If?" How this formula works in relation to your problem is to write down the answers to "What if I do this, this way?" or "What if I do it that way to solve a problem?" You should continue thinking of different ways and possibilities to solve the problem that you are most concerned with at a particular time and write down all the possibilities on a list. You will then have a few possible solutions to your most pressing problem and should choose the best possible answer from your list – the one that makes the most sense for solving that problem – and see where that takes you.

You could try any other problem solving techniques that you may know or maybe you could even use your vivid imagination to solve problems. Now after attempting problem solving techniques you may have shifted from being a problem maker to being a problem solver in the process. After all, "It's better to be a problem solver than a problem maker."

WISDOM FROM THE AGES - XXXIV

*"If WEALTH IS LOST, NOTHING IS LOST; IF
HEALTH IS LOST, SOMETHING IS LOST; BUT IF
CHARACTER IS LOST, EVERYTHING IS LOST"*

Interpretation: This is a comparison of loss of wealth, loss of health and loss of character. However, the point being made is that if you lose your character, you lose your integrity. Your character defines your personality, so if your personality is lost, all is lost.

"Avoid The Jealous and Envious People Pretending to Be a Friend Disease"

There is no vaccine for this disease.

There're probably not many people in the world today that will admit to having the jealous and envious disease, but you can spot them by using your sense of discernment or by their behavior and actions or inactions. The jealous and envious people will pretend to be your friend and even smile in your face. At certain times, it may be easy to spot them, because they will go as far as to compliment you with a grimacing smile but won't support you on a damn thing. All they might do is talk with you, without any actions to help your cause. They will tell you that you are right but secretly wishing you were wrong. However, ironically, the jealous and envious persons will want you to show support for them and their endeavors, while they secretly want you to fail. Even people you know that was a good friend at one time are susceptible of contracting the jealous and envious disease, and they may secretly work against your best interests and hate on your minor successes. We say *minor* successes because maintaining a decent standard of living for yourself is minor in the grand scheme of things, but these types of characters are evidently small minds at work.

So, be mindful of them and minimize your interactions with the jealous and envious people that circulate within your circle of trust. Even some family members may contract this disease.

You will sometimes be able to recognize the diseased individuals by their facial expressions, like the half smiles, the general look of a bad attitude showing on their face, and also the vibes you get from them. It's possible that they may be wearing a mask now in an attempt to deceive you later.

WISDOM FROM THE AGES - XXXV

"SOMETIMES PEOPLE WILL
PUT UP A FALSE FLAG"

Interpretation: An intentional misrepresentation of someone's allegiance. Some people may try to make you think they are a friend when, in fact they are a foe.

"Do The Right Thing"

"Do the Right Thing" is a catchphrase that is popular in American culture. Many people have been raised from childhood to adulthood to "Do the Right Thing" in all circumstances according to their judgement.

However, as adults, we have become more mature than we were during childhood. So, many people may have realized that "doing the right thing" may not always be correct for every situation. Knowing that our thinking has evolved, we realize that we should always do what's best for a given situation as opposed to doing what we *think* is the right thing to do, because doing the right thing is subjective to each individual.

Please understand that there can be a significant difference between doing the right thing and doing what is best for a situation.

You should be fully aware by now that "doing the right thing" may not always coincide with doing what is best. You may have experienced situations in which you decided to do the right thing and found out later that what you thought was the right thing did not turn out to be the best thing for that situation.

So, hopefully you understand the distinction being made here between "doing the right thing" and doing what is best for the situation.

Common sense dictates that doing what is best for a situation is more prudent than "doing the right thing." However, this concept can still be debatable among some people because "Do the Right Thing" is a more popular catchphrase compared to doing what is "best" for a situation.

WISDOM FROM THE AGES - XXXVI

"EXPERIENCE IS THE BEST
TEACHER IN THE WORLD"

Interpretation: It's self explanatory.

"Warning: Avoid The Confidently Ignorant People Among Us"

Everyone has the right to remain ignorant; it's a choice of their free will. It's an altogether different situation to be confidently ignorant. It's bad enough to be ignorant, but to have confidence with the ignorance is a problem on top of a problem. It is an uphill battle trying to get a person who is confidently ignorant to become aware of their condition. A standard quote of many confidently ignorant people is: "I know what I'm talking about" (repeat that statement as quickly as they would). They may go on to express their views and say, "I don't need a book, pencil or paper to prove me right," or "What in the hell are you trying to say to me?"

Here is where the problem lies: this type of character doesn't think of earning creditability and respect from other people they come into contact with. They may think that they don't have to prove that they are of good character; indeed, they may be oblivious as to what good character really is. So, should you spend your precious time trying to help them see reality for what it is when that individual has already decided that they are right in whatever they say or do, regardless of the situation and circumstances? You might as well move on because it's not worth your time to try to get a confidently ignorant person to become aware of their condition.

Once you recognize these character traits in a person and the brazen attitude that they may have, you'll know who you are dealing with.

"Warning: avoid the confidently ignorant people among us" because if someone notices you arguing with this type of individual and you are both going back and forth yelling while trying to have a conversation, the third party may not know which one of you has the problem of being confidently ignorant.

It's bad enough to be ignorant, but to have confidence with the ignorance is another situation altogether.

WISDOM FROM THE AGES - XXXVII

*"THE MORE EDUCATED YOU BECOME, THE
MORE DOCILE YOU MAY BECOME ACCORDING
TO THE WESTERN WORLD VIEW"*

Interpretation: It's self explanatory.

"Some People Are Too Damn Lazy to Think for Themselves"

It sounds almost impossible to believe that someone could be too lazy to think for themselves. Thinking does take effort sometimes, but, on other occasions, thinking about certain matters can be almost automatic, with no long-term thinking required.

You've probably noticed that certain people seem too lazy to think things through on the simplest of tasks that could benefit them personally. Their issue could be either that they just don't feel like forcing their mind to concentrate on the matter at hand, or that they don't feel in the mood (a moody person) to follow a certain train of thought to its conclusion. So, it may be easier for them to believe that they can't do it without trying to think things through on their own, when, in fact, it could be the simplest of tasks to complete.

Common sense dictates that each individual should think for themselves, although some people prefer to allow someone else to do the thinking for them as it's easier. So, it's not always that people don't have the aptitude or ability to think for themselves. It's just that, sometimes, certain people are too damn lazy to think for themselves.

WISDOM FROM THE AGES - XXXVIII

*"COMMON SENSE IS NOT ALWAYS COMMON TO
ALL PEOPLE, IN ALL CIRCUMSTANCES"*

Interpretation: It's self explanatory.

"You Just Got a Bought-and-Paid-for Lesson in Life"

The statement above infers a common sense understanding when you attempt to decipher its meaning.

An example of "you just got a bought-and-paid-for lesson in life" would be a person trying very hard to pursue a particular career path with constant adversity. Then, one day, he or she is faced with a crude awakening. They may realize that this course of action is not going to work for him or her. Thereafter, the individual may bemoan all of the time and money spent on this particular endeavor when they realize they're on the wrong path.

However, each person must learn this type of lesson for themselves and realize when it is definitely time to move on.

Another example is subtitled, "A Mother's Love is the Strongest Love on the Planet." A mother may try her hardest to get her son to be a productive and responsible man. The mother may try everything within her power to keep her son safe and, above all, to make him a productive and responsible man. The mother may go to the limit to pay for her adult son's needs and wants with the hope that he will mature to the point of being productive and responsible. However, what certain mothers don't realize sometimes is that her man-child has to want to be productive and responsible for himself. If he doesn't want it for himself, it may not happen. Still, the mother continues to support her man-child to the point that she gets humiliated in the process and totally mortified, too.

There is an extreme range of situations that may cause these circumstances to occur. Some situations like this may even escalate to the point that the mother could be arrested because of certain actions that her man-child has caused. Furthermore, the mother could also possibly spend all of her money on her man-child's needs to the point that she doesn't have enough money for her own basic essential items. All of this may happen in a flash of time and the mother may be faced with a life-defining moment, because she relentlessly continues to do all that she can for her man-child while he continues to exhibit negative behavior. She may experience a final heartbreak with her man-child. After all, she may realize one day that she has been aiding and abetting her grown son with his misconduct. The mother may realize one day that her son has to want to be responsible and productive for his own good in life.

Henceforth, the mother may be faced one day with the reality that she just got a bought-and-paid-for lesson in life. She may then immediately realize that she bought this lesson with her own money, which was spent supporting her man-child. She may also see that she paid for this life lesson with the time and energy that she put into her man-child only to get to this point of final heartbreak.

The moral of this story is that you must realize A.S.A.P. when "you just got a bought-and-paid-for lesson in life," and this can apply to many different situations and circumstances in life.

WISDOM FROM THE AGES - XXXIX

*"VIGILANTIBUS NON DORMIENTIBUS
JURA SUBVENIUNT"*

Interpretation: The law assists those who are vigilant, not those who sleep over their rights.

"The Ultimate Step in Every Decision Making Process"

The formula for making important decisions can be simple sometimes. However, when you were a child, you thought the method you used for decision making was intense – it was "eenie-meenie-miney-moe." Do you remember?

Thereafter, you were taught in primary school to make decisions based on a process called "weighing the pros against the cons" (comparing the positives against the negatives and vice-versa).

Now, in adulthood, you may have learned to use knowledge, understanding, research and facts, along with "weighing the pros against the cons." However, you must go one step further in your decision-making process and it should be the ultimate step in every decision you make. You should always check within yourself, within your individual spirit/intuition, to realize how you feel about the outcome of "weighing the pros against the cons" alongside all other pertinent information that may be relevant in the process.

So, in essence, you are checking how you feel (yes or no) spiritually about the overall matter, which you have decided on already. This ultimate step happens only after your deliberation process has been completed.

.

WISDOM FROM THE AGES - XL

"REMIND YOURSELF DAILY THAT YOU ARE A SPIRITUAL BEING HAVING A PHYSICAL EXPERIENCE AND REGARDLESS OF THE ISSUES OF THE DAY, THAT YOU ARE STILL ON A SWEET AND WONDERFUL JOURNEY, A.K.A. LIFE."

Interpretation: It's self explanatory.

"You Are The Hero That You Have Been Waiting For"

No one is going to save you, no miracle, no lucky break, not even your savior. However, before you spiral out of control into despair, you must realize that this may be the best News that you may ever come to know. Because, once you really realize that no one is ever going to save you, then that can only mean one thing, that you must save yourself. So, stop waiting secretly for something good to happen for you from out of the sky..

The sooner you man up and take full responsibility for your future and realize that you don't have to wait for someone else's approval or someone else's permission, then you will have given yourself the power that you need to move forward and grant yourself permission and approval to make your next move, even if your not really sure what it is. These particular actions will make you feel liberated even if it doesn't work out as you may have planned, this type of power can make you feel good and that's a win.

When you realize that you have the power then you won't have to wait for someone else to believe in you, you won't have to wait for someone to see your worth, because you'll feel that it's within your control.

At this point, the only thing left to do is to take action in one direction or another, you decide, however take action or make a move every day that you can, until you notice some type of results from your actions and build on it from there. Because, no one is going to save you, "You Are The Hero That You Have Been Waiting For."

Conclusion

As mentioned in the introduction, the subject of common sense is so vast and expansive in and of itself that we can only humanly examine an incremental amount of key common sense concepts that are of importance and which may be familiar to you when it comes to understanding common sense in general. With that information being stated, this book is perhaps the most comprehensive book on the subject matter of motivational common sense available today.

It must be recognized that from one generation to the next, common sense has been taught by way of old adages (old sayings) and life experiences. The old adages were repeated repetitiously and then paraphrased several times to get the message across to the person willing to listen and learn the lesson. In this book, some of the key common sense concepts are available and transformed into common sense codes along with the old adages for a clear, concise understanding of common sense terms and phrases. You can now read the common sense concepts written herein until you learn, understand and digest them. This book has provided a much easier method to learn common sense than the repetitive process that previous generations had to endure. It's a proven fact that some learn faster by reading information compared to listening to the same information.

An additional benefit of reading this book is that it may allow you an opportunity to grasp more widely accepted common sense concepts, because the common sense codes have a variety of different subject matter that you may or may not be familiar with. However, you will learn many other facts and some consciousness raising information while still concentrating on learning more about the main subject of common sense.

This book offers you a broader view of common sense concepts as compared to Grandma's brand of common sense ("Look both ways when crossing the street," for example). The concept of common sense has been revised and expanded to the point of being considered to be a part of the category of consciousness. Today, an individual who has common sense can become more aware of the world that we live in by having a much broader scope of common sense. So, to possess common sense today can be more beneficial to you than some college degrees, because it can be more advantageous for you to increase your understanding of common sense than it is to increase your intellect. Case and point: a master's degree won't tell you which way to go, but common sense will.

Once you can understand and see the value in the variety of subjects selected for each individual code and understand the point in each common sense code and old adage, you may begin to think in a more deep and profound manner. This is a possible avenue that you could approach many circumstances in your life, by trying to find the common sense point of view in each situation you encounter. You should always think about asking yourself if what is being said or done make common sense and then seek answers to those questions. This practice will help you to develop in the area of a common sense understanding. This practice of asking yourself these questions is a key point in learning to understand and use common sense as a daily practice and guide.

So, you should use this very valuable consciousness raising information within these common sense codes and old adages (wisdom from the ages), along with your friends and family members, too. Because some people may or may not be completely clear on many of the common sense concepts that are available today. So, determine for yourself how this book, *The Common Sense Code Guide With Wisdom From The Ages Volume - I: Illumination*, has helped you or someone you know gain a better understanding of common sense..

You must know that understanding is one of the most important faculties in your mind and having a good understanding of common sense is essential to guiding your life.

About The Author

Currently residing in Washington, DC, author Malik El finds immense interest in studying world renowned leaders and philosophers. Among all, his favorite philosopher remains his mother, the late Martha Whitehead Gordon, whose wise words and insights have always guided him, despite her limited formal education. His passion for history and decoding hidden truths often leads him to archives and national museums, where he delves into the past to bring clarity to the present.

Born and raised in New Jersey, Malik El has always possessed an insatiable curiosity about human intuition. This cultivation of a sense of awareness has been a guiding force, helping him to navigate the complexities of life and avoid the pitfalls lurking nearby. In addition to his philosophical pursuits, Malik El has a background in broadcasting, having hosted a popular radio show in Atlanta, GA. His extensive travels have broadened his horizons, enriched his understanding of diverse cultures, and brought a wealth of experience and perspective to his writing.

For the past three years, Malik El has been dedicated to compiling his life lessons into a format that others can easily grasp and benefit from. His inspiration to write stems from a deep rooted tradition of passing down knowledge, driven by a desire to fill the void in literature on the study of life, specifically the concept of motivational common sense. His work is a testament to his belief in the power of shared wisdom and the enduring legacy of thoughtful reflection and family values.

When he's not writing, Malik El is a businessman and can often be found exploring new ideas, volunteering in his community, and immersing himself in the rich history of his surroundings.

Connect with him on Facebook and LinkedIn or visit his website at www. commonsensecodeguide.com.

.

www.ingramcontent.com/pod-product-compliance
Lightning Source LLC
Chambersburg PA
CBHW051216120626
46547CB00013B/1382